Healthy Eating

Milk and Cheese

Nancy Dickmann

Raintree

www.raintreepublishers.co.uk
Visit our website to find out
more information about
Raintree books.

To order:

☎ Phone 0845 6044371

🖹 Fax +44 (0) 1865 312263

🖳 Email myorders@raintreepublishers.co.uk

Customers from outside the UK please telephone +44 1865 312262

Raintree is an imprint of Capstone Global Library Limited, a company incorporated in England and Wales having its registered office at 7 Pilgrim Street, London, EC4V 6LB – Registered company number: 6695582

Edited by Sian Smith, Nancy Dickmann, and Rebecca Rissman
Designed by Joanna Hinton-Malivoire
Original Illustrations © Capstone Global Library Ltd 2010
Illustrated by Tony Wilson
Picture research by Elizabeth Alexander
Production by Victoria Fitzgerald
Originated by Capstone Global Library Ltd
Printed and bound in China by South China Printing Company Ltd

ISBN 978 0 431 00540 9 (hardback)
14 13 12 11 10
10 9 8 7 6 5 4 3 2 1

ISBN 978 0 431 00993 3 (paperback)
15 14 13 12 11
10 9 8 7 6 5 4 3 2 1

British Library Cataloguing in Publication Data
Dickmann, Nancy.
   Milk and cheese. -- (Healthy eating)
   1. Dairy products--Juvenile literature. 2. Dairy products
   in human nutrition--Juvenile literature.
   I. Title II. Series
   641.3'7-dc22

Acknowledgements
We would like to thank the following for permission to reproduce photographs: © Capstone Publishers p.**22** (Karon Dubke); Alamy p.**15** (© Cultura); Corbis pp.**18**, **23 bottom** (© Bernd Vogel), **21** (© moodboard); Food Standards Agency/ © Crown copyright material is reproduced with the permission of the Controller of HMSO and Queen's Printer for Scotland p.**17**; Getty Images pp.**7** (Gavriel Jecan/The Image Bank), **19** (Dave King/ Dorling Kindersley); Getty Images/Digital Vision p.**14** (Christopher Robbins); iStockphoto pp.**20**, **13** (© Rosemarie Gearhart), p**23 top** (© Mark Hatfield); Photolibrary pp.**5** (Hans Huber/Westend61), **8** (Maximilian Stock LTD/ Phototake Science), **11** (Willy De L'Horme/Photononstop), **12** (Kablonk!), **16** (Banana Stock); Shutterstock pp.**4** (© Chepko Danil Vitalevich), **6** (© Viorel Sima), **9** (© Morgan Lane Photography), **10** (© matka_Wariatka).

Front cover photograph of milk and dairy products reproduced with permission of © Capstone Publishers (Karon Dubke). Back cover photograph reproduced with permission of Shutterstock (© Viorel Sima).

We would like to thank Dr Sarah Schenker for her invaluable help in the preparation of this book.

Every effort has been made to contact copyright holders of material reproduced in this book. Any omissions will be rectified in subsequent printings if notice is given to the publishers.

Contents

What is milk?

Milk is a drink that is made by some animals.

Drinking milk helps keep us healthy.

Most of our milk comes from cows.

goats

Some of our milk comes from goats.

Food from milk

cheese

Milk can be made into other foods.

These foods are called dairy foods.

Cheese is made from milk.

Yoghurt is made from milk.

How milk helps us

Milk and dairy foods help build strong bones.

Milk and dairy foods help build strong teeth.

Milk and dairy foods help your body grow.

Milk and dairy foods help keep your blood healthy.

Healthy eating

We need to eat different kinds of food each day.

milk and dairy foods

The eatwell plate shows us which foods to eat.

cheese

Some dairy foods have a lot of fat.

You should only eat a little of these foods.

We eat milk and dairy foods to stay healthy.

We eat milk and dairy foods because they taste good!

Find the dairy food

Here is a healthy dinner. Can you find two foods made from milk?

Answer on page 24

Picture glossary

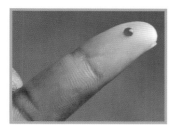 **blood** red liquid inside your body. Blood takes food and air to all your body parts.

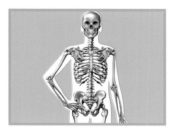 **bones** you have bones inside your body. Bones are strong and hard. They help to keep your body up.

 **fat** oily thing in some foods. Your body uses fat to keep warm. Eating too much fat is bad for your body.

Index

Answer to quiz on page 22: The cheese and the yoghurt are made from milk.

Notes for parents and teachers

Before reading

Explain that we need to eat a range of different foods to stay healthy. Splitting foods into different groups can help us understand how much food we should eat from each group. Introduce the milk and dairy foods section of the plate on page 17. These foods give us calcium which helps build strong teeth and bones. Explain that some people are allergic to milk and dairy products. They can get the calcium they need through special foods such as soya milk, which is made from soya beans (this appears on the eatwell plate).

After reading

- Brainstorm different dairy foods as a class. Explain that some dairy foods are high in fat and we need to be careful not to eat too much of these. Show the foods high in fat or sugar section of the plate on page 17, and point out that butter is in this section. Together, highlight butter and any other dairy foods in the list that can be high in fat or sugar, such as cheese and ice cream.

- Show how milk can be turned into butter. Fill a clear, lidded jar half full with heavy cream. Take turns shaking the jar. After about 20–30 minutes a lump of butter should form along with a liquid. Pour the liquid buttermilk into a separate container and wash the butter under cold water until the water runs clear. Taste the butter on wholemeal bread or crackers.

- Help the children to make posters encouraging people to try milk and dairy foods. Use the posters to show why we need milk and dairy foods to help us build strong teeth and bones and to stay healthy.